OVERCOMING OBSTACLES

OVERCOMING OBSTACLES

30 DAY DEVOTIONAL

Jayda T. James

Printed in the United States of America
Library of Congress Cataloging in Publication Data

ISBN: 9781797788128

Dedication

This book is dedicated to anyone like me, who has been confused, hurt, or in search of better . It is also dedicated to my husband, William, for his lasting love and support.

DAY

1

DOUBT

Trust in the LORD with all thine heart; and lean not unto thine own understanding. In all thy ways acknowledge him, and he shall direct thy paths.7 Be not wise in thine own eyes: fear the LORD, and depart from evil. It shall be health to thy navel, and marrow to thy bones.
(Proverbs 3:5-8, KJV)

We doubt ourselves all the time. There are these voices that play over and over in our head, telling us what we cannot do. There are those people around us that constantly tell us we will not be successful for whatever reason. However, the above verse tells us that we cannot trust what those voices or other people are telling us; we cannot even trust ourselves! We must put our faith and trust in the Lord believing him for the promises we have already been granted.

What doubts do you have? There is something you want....something you want to do. Why have you not pursued it yet?

Take about 10 minutes to think and write about where this doubt is coming from. Be sure to conclude this journal entry with how you plan to combat this doubt and remove it from your thoughts. This SOMETHING that you desire will seem closer to your grasp once you remove the doubt!

I Am An Overcomer

DAY

2

FEAR

Fear thou not; for I am with thee: be not dismayed; for I am thy God: I willstrengthen thee; yea, I will help thee; yea, I will uphold thee with the right hand of my righteousness. (Isaiah 41:10, KJV)

I have heard fear being described as false evidence appearing real. There are things that we see, hear, feel, touch, smell, and taste that evoke this feeling of fear. It is because we can see, hear, feel, touch, smell, or taste it that there is evidence of its existence. But it is actually false because there is no real basis that whatever this thing is can actually hurt you. God tells you in the above verse that all your strength and help comes from Him.....the most powerful being! If God is holding you in His right hand and blessing the Universe with His left, whatever this thing is that you are afraid of means nothing. It cannot hurt or harm you unless you give it the power to do so!

What are you afraid of? Take some time to think about your biggest fear.

Write it down and decide today that you will no longer be afraid of this thing. You need to think about how you will no longer feed into the energy of this thing by thinking about it and resting in it. Conclude this entry with where you will pull the strength and motivation from to combat this fear and overcome it!

I Am An Overcomer

3

OBSTACLES

More than that, we rejoice in our sufferings, knowing that suffering produces endurance, and endurance produces character, and character produces hope, and hope does not put us to shame, because God's love has been poured into our hearts through the Holy Spirit who has been given to us. (Romans 3:3-5, KJV)

Obstacles are hurdles but I have seen those that are properly trained jump over hurdles. You may think well they are athletes and they practice that sporting event every day. Guess what? You are an athlete in life and you practice every day! You need strength, endurance, routine, and practice to reach that level of success and victory that people around you experience all the time. The above verse is confirmation from God's Word that when you suffer, you grow. You grow as a person and your character increases. Your character is what attracts you to other people.

Think about a current obstacle you are facing. Write what it is and why you think you have been faced with this obstacle. How is this obstacle going to produce character in you?

As you conclude this entry, be sure to include the hope you feel as a result of facing this obstacle. The more you think about this, focus on what will come out of it more than what it is right now!

I Am An Overcomer

DAY 4

INSECURITY

I will praise thee; for I am fearfully and wonderfully made: marvellous are thyworks; and that my soul knoweth right well.
(Psalm 139:14, KJV)

Insecurities come from us.....we create them, not God! If we can shift our mindset and adopt the Word of God then we stand a better chance at success. Whatever you are insecure about, you can overcome that with a change in the way you think. What types of thoughts are you allowing to come into your mind? If you can accept that you are indeed made in the image of God, then you are accepting your own power to control the outcome of your life. You will even begin to avoid careless choices because your thoughts are managed by God!

What insecurities do you have? Write them down and then write LIES. Whatever you feel inadequate about is a lie because someone else fostered that inside you. Now that you have removed that, you have room to focus on what is important.

Write three things that make you absolutely wonderful. Once you believe in yourself, you have the ability to achieve the great things you were meant to!

I Am An Overcomer

DAY 5

RELATIONSHIPS

Wherefore comfort yourselves together, and edify one another,
even as also ye do.
(1 Thessalonians 5:11, KJV)

As you work on yourself, your relationships with those around you are going to change; some for the better and some for the worse. I say the better because there will be people that enter your life completely by divine intervention. God is going to set these relationships up because they serve a purpose toward the personal goals you have set for yourself. I say the worse because everyone that knows you will not understand the changes going on with you. Due to the fact that you are growing and evolving, those that have known the former you will not quite know what to do with these changes. They may accept them or not. The verse above states we must encourage one another. Anyone that is not building you up may not be necessary!

Write a prayer in your journal. Ask God to enhance your ability to recognize those that are for you and those that are not serving a true purpose in your life at this time. This prayer will be one that could very well bring about emotions that have the possibility to take you backward. However, backward is not the direction you are destined to go in......forward motion only!

I Am An Overcomer

DAY

6

INTERACTIONS WITH PEOPLE

A new commandment I give unto you, That ye love one another; as I have loved you, that ye also love one another.
By this shall all men know that ye are my disciples, if ye have love one to another.
(John 13:35-36, KJV)

Every person that you come in contact with will not be "relationship material" but that does not mean you will not have to interact with them. Relationships involve dealing with another person despite what their faults may be because you love them. How you interact with other people helps you define your character and how other people treat you. The above verse gives the key to positive interactions with people and that is LOVE. God loved us enough to give the life of His only son so that we may live on this Earth with one another in peace showing love to each other. How are you going to interact with the people you come in contact with on a daily basis?

Journal about how you are going to show love; especially when the person you are interacting with is not someone you actually love. The person could be anyone but what God commands us to do is show love toward one another just as He showed us love by allowing His son to die on a cross.As you journal, think about how important this is when it comes to fostering positive relationships in your life.

I Am An Overcomer

DAY

7

ACCOUNTABILITY

So then every one of us shall give account of himself to God.
(Romans 14:12, KJV)

Accountability is hard because we tend to justify when and how we fall short. And we most certainly do not want anyone telling us that we are wrong or should be doing more or doing something different. So if this is the case, how do you hold yourself accountable for what you do, when you do it, or how you do it, especially when it is not your best? You have to be honest with yourself. Do not beat yourself up but believe enough in yourself to know that even if you are wrong or have messed up that the mess up is to make you stronger. You must learn from it to become stronger.

You know that you cannot hide your mistakes from God. It is time to journal about a time that you did one thing but should have done something different. This is a time when you did not hold yourself accountable for your own actions. Now that you know better, you can do better. If this is a situation you can still change, that is even better.

However, if it is not, you need to write how you would have done things differently, perhaps in a more productive way. This entry will allow you to reflect and maybe even forgive yourself for a past action for which now you can be held accountable.

I Am An Overcomer

DAY

8

But the fruit of the Spirit is love, joy, peace, longsuffering, gentleness,goodness, faith, Meekness, temperance: against such there is no law.
(Galatians 5:22-23, KJV)

We should all be holding ourselves accountable based on the principles by which we live. The above scripture lays out in plain verse the principles that are expected of us. What we expect from others is exactly what we should be displaying ourselves. Of course this is not always the outcome because we are human and subject to error, but we have to use our principles to guide us as we go through our lives every day.

Journal about how you plan to use the fruit of the Spirit more. How will you show these? How will you recognize and respond to them? The objective is to not only be able to give them but to accept them as well.

I Am An Overcomer

DAY

9

DECISIONS

Teach me thy way, O LORD; I will walk in thy truth:
unite my heart to fear thy name.
(Psalm 86:11, KJV)

We make decisions every day! The amount of decisions we make depends greatly on the lifestyle we live. Some of us are parents, have demanding jobs, are married, are dating, are taking care of loved ones, or just trying to make life work. Decisions can be made out of frustration or aggravation and that usually never works. When we have to make a decision, we have to make sure it is based on a process; a thought process that allows you to consider the consequences prior to having to face them.

Think about a big decision you have to make soon. Whatever it is, write about it and as you do, pray! Ask God to help guide the thoughts that will lead to your ultimate decision.

You do not have to necessarily write down the final decision but once it is made, use this particular entry to see how it affected the outcome.

I Am An Overcomer

DAY

10

Casting all your care upon him; for he careth for you.
(1 Peter 5:7, KJV)

You have overcome something! If not, it is coming. That is not to scare you but we all have a moment in life where we have to overcome something that results in us being stronger and better. Overcoming things in life really means that you have faced something that has tested you; tested your patience and your faith. In order to feel as though you have passed this test, you look at it from the perspective of what you have gained even though you may feel as if you have lost.

What have you overcome? You have faced something hard and difficult in your life and your challenge is to write about it. This may be something that you have never told anyone about; something that has been extremely hurtful.

Whatever it is, you have to be able to see it as something that has not defeated you but instead made you stronger. This has the potential to be emotionally draining but important enough so that you can feel a sense of truly overcoming!

I Am An Overcomer

DAY

11

POSSIBILITIES

"But he that shall endure unto the end, the same shall be saved."
(Matthew 24:13, KJV)

You have heard people say that the possibilities are endless. I only believe this is true if we have put our trust in God. When you are facing a difficult situation you have to be able to see the end of it. Being able to see an outcome is understanding the possibilities. A difficult situation does not last a lifetime and you have to see it to the end; you cannot stop fighting. The above verse offers a sense of hope in that if you are able to endure, you experience an outcome that could bring you to the next level.

Think about an obstacle you are facing. While this obstacle may seem like you cannot overcome it, please consider the possibilities that could be a result of you experiencing this situation. If you are able to do this, it could help you focus on the end of it even while you are in the midst of it.

I Am An Overcomer

DAY

12

POWER

"For God hath not given us the spirit of fear; but of power, and of love, and of a sound mind."
(2 Timothy 1:7, KJV)

Who does not desire power? We all want it and we go about different ways of obtaining it. Having power means to some of us that we are in control. Being in control may mean that no one can manipulate you or tell you what to do. Well, too much power can actually take you out of control. Power must be maintained and the most powerful person has to be able to relinquish power when and to whom it is necessary. Do you consider yourself powerful?

Think about where you feel most powerful in your life. Is it at your job? Perhaps you are the "boss". Is it at home? Perhaps you determine the rules. Is it in your relationship? Perhaps you control the path your relationship with your significant other is taking. Now think about where you feel least powerful. Is it your job, home, or relationship?

Write about where you feel most and least powerful and figure out how you need these to change or stay the same.

I Am An Overcomer

DAY 13

TRANQUILITY

"Be careful for nothing; but in every thing by prayer and supplication with thanksgiving let your requests be made known unto God. And the peace of God, which passeth all understanding, shall keep your hearts and minds through Christ Jesus."
(Philippians 4:6-7, KJV)

Tranquility is synonymous with peace, and who do you know that does not desire peace? I am not sure what comes to your mind when you think of peace, but I think of that moment when chaos and despair are all around me and I can still smile and thank God. Peace is a state of mind. These verses help us to understand that we do not have to worry about anything because we have prayer. We are only human so we will have anxieties from time to time, however, being children of the most High God grants us the ability to come to Him in prayer with total thanksgiving in our hearts.

There is something on your mind right now that may be causing you some angst. You have been thinking about how you are going to be at peace with this. The tranquility you seek is closer than you think!

Write a short prayer right now asking God to free you from the anxiety or worry you may feel. As you conclude your prayer, remember to ask for clarity so that you are able to think clearly enough so that when God speaks, you can hear Him.

I Am An Overcomer

DAY

14

FREEDOM

"Stand fast therefore in the liberty wherewith Christ hath made us free, and be not entangled again with the yoke of bondage."
(Galatians 5:1, KJV)

Usually when one thinks of freedom, they may think of slavery or being enslaved because freedom is associated with captivity. The ultimate freedom lies in your mind. If you think about slaves and slavery, it was about control of the mind. An entire race of people were able to be captured and enslaved because their minds were controlled. Fear was able to settle in because of the thoughts that went through their minds. The only reason so many people are enslaved today and cannot experience a true sense of freedom is because of what they have allowed to enter their minds. Your thoughts control and oftentimes enslave you. Allow God to be the center of your thoughts and you become free!

What thoughts do you have that stop you from being free? These thoughts are negative and pessimistic. It does not matter who put them there, they exist and should not. Decide to be free today.

Write what freedom means to you. As you write about it, think about how this looks in your life. Be sure to include how you plan to achieve this freedom.

I Am An Overcomer

DAY

15

NEGATIVITY

"There hath no temptation taken you but such as is common to man: but God is faithful, who will not suffer you to be tempted above that ye are able; but will with the temptation also make a way to escape, that ye may be able to bear it."
(1 Corinthians 10:13, KJV)

We all know negative people.....you may be the negative person someone knows! While negativity is not helping your glowing personality, it has roots in people who have suffered from this demon for a long time. Regardless of how long you have endured, thank God there is a way out. The above verse tells us that God is faithful. This means that negativity is around you and may even be in you but God gives you the power to recognize it and the desire to want to escape it. If you have reached a point in your life where you say to yourself, and maybe even others, that you no longer want this negativity around or in you, you are listening to God and opening your mind and spirit to the better that exists for us.

You will not be able to avoid negativity just because you are a good person. Everyone you come in contact with will not be at the same level as you, but your involvement with them is meant to make you stronger after the encounter is over.

Write about the negativity you have had to face lately. Who is it that is negative? Is it you? If so, it is okay because you are taking a major step toward escaping. As you conclude this entry, write about how this negativity will no longer hold a place in your life. There will be no room!

I Am An Overcomer

16

CONFUSION

"Consider what I say; and the Lord give thee understanding in all things."
(2 Timothy 2:7, KJV)

There is nothing more intolerable than confusion. No one likes to feel confused about anyone or anything. Confusion leads to assumption and assumption leads to the belief of lies. It is a very vicious cycle of deception that confusion has and when we practice walking in it, we can never have a clear spirit. As a leader in this life, you cannot operate in confusion. You will not be effective in your communication which will lead to ineffective leadership. You may not think you are a leader but you are and you must create practices and habits that make room for healthy and positive thinking.

Think about the last time you were honestly confused. Was it something that was said? Or perhaps it was the way someone treated you?

Write about that time and the other feelings that resulted from it. Be sure to include how you plan to avoid this feeling in your future. You do not have to be associated with it and soon people will know not to bring it your way.

I Am An Overcomer

DAY 17

ENDURANCE

"Blessed is the man that endureth temptation: for when he is tried, he shall receive the crown of life, which the Lord hath promised to them that love him."
(James 1:12, KJV)

The ability to endure builds character. You endure the pain and hardships of life to make you better, not worse. When we think of some of the worst things we have had to endure, we shake our heads and wonder how we got through it. We hear of people's stories of having to endure incredibly horrible situations or circumstances and we are in awe. The word "temptation" as used in the above verse has nothing to do with sex or infidelity but ANYTHING that has the ability to make you turn from your growth in Christ. Being able to endure some of the most painful moments in life bring about some of the greatest blessings!

In all honesty, you do not run from hardship and pain; you embrace it and look to God to help you figure out the blessings that are to come from enduring. God provides these opportunities for us to be more humble and wise.

Write about a time you, or someone you know, had to endure something painful, traumatic, horrible. It may be too painful to relive in words but write about the pain. What have you seen in yourself, or the other person, as a result of it? What has being able to endure the pain taught you?

I Am An Overcomer

DAY

18

REVELATION

"That the God of our Lord Jesus Christ, the Father of glory, may give unto you the spirit of wisdom and revelation in the knowledge of him."
(Ephesians 1:17, KJV)

When I think of revelation, I think of clarity. Revelation comes after confusion. After confusion, all things become clear and actually make sense; it finally comes together. Perhaps that is why this is the name of the last book of the Bible. God's Word is filled with everything we need; history, stories, teachings, rules, examples....all we can use to help guide us and keep us sane. Revelation comes with a clear mind and a clear mind is the result of allowing God to be at the center of our thoughts and actions. Just imagine the amount of wisdom that comes along with thinking clearly and being mindful of your surroundings! It is time for revelation!

You have been living in a mist long enough. It is time to come out of the clouds so that all things can be revealed. Why is revelation important to you?

Write about revelation and what it means to you. Why is this such a milestone in this journey in which you have chosen to take? As you conclude this entry, be mindful of the amount of wisdom you will have once you fully acknowledge the power of God in your life.

I Am An Overcomer

DAY

19

TRUTH

"Jesus saith unto him, I am the way, the truth, and the life:
no man cometh unto the Father, but by me."
(John 14:6, KJV)

Most people are now "walking in their truth" or "living their truth" but the only issue with this is you are now projecting your truth onto others. Your truth belongs to you as my truth belongs to me. The verse tells us that Jesus Christ was the only true and honest person to walk this Earth. You do not get to God telling YOUR truth....but by telling OTHER PEOPLE the truth about Jesus Christ. Living your truth will be whatever you need it to be. As a Christian person, your obligation is to God and telling the truth about Him.

Did you know there are three things that God CANNOT do? It is true!

Try to discover what these are and write them down. It may take a while and that is okay, but once you discover them, be sure to include why you are thankful that God cannot do these things. Discover the truth so you can spread the good news!

I Am An Overcomer

DAY

20

STRENGTH

"I can do all things through Christ which strengtheneth me."
(Philippians 4:13, KJV)

We ask for strength every day. We need strength to handle situations, people, and circumstances. There are things that happen to us all throughout the day that test our strength. The extreme nature of circumstances can sometimes be so overwhelming. We can go from extreme happiness to extreme sadness in a matter of seconds. Where does one find the strength to be able to handle such a vast amount of emotion in such a short period of time? The above verse tells you exact! We live because of Christ Jesus. If you think back over some of your situations and circumstances, you marvel at your own tenacity! You ask, "How did I get through that?" God has equipped and enabled you to handle a multitude of situations. All that you rely on has come from Christ.

Think about a time when you got through something and had no idea how. What was it and how do you know it had to be due to the strength of a higher power?

I Am An Overcomer

21

SUCCESS

"Humble yourselves in the sight of the Lord, and he shall lift you up."
(James 4:10, KJV)

You would be lying to yourself if you said you did not want to be successful. But success looks different for each of us so what you cannot do is try to establish your level of success based on what you see happening in someone else's life. This is not an easy task because you have to look at multiple aspects of your life. How will success look in each of those areas? The above verse lets us know that in order to be successful, humility is necessary. Success is exaltation from God and your relationship with God is different from others therefore your success being different as well.

How do you view success? What does being successful look like for you? Being successful for you may be having a family or having that perfect job. Think about what you want in your life and why you may not have it yet.

Write about what success is for you. As you write, think about the things you want. Some of them you have already and some you have yet to obtain. In your conclusion, include how being humble plays a part in you being successful.

I Am An Overcomer

DAY

22

HUMILITY

"By humility and the fear of the Lord are riches, and honor, and life."
(Proverbs 22:4, KJV)

There are so many people who do not understand humility. They do not know how to display humility without feeling like others are interpreting it as something else. How others interpret your actions is not really important. It is what you are doing and how you are treating other people that is most relevant. If you read the above verse, you see the words riches, honor, and life.....who does not want these? I sure do! Now look at the two things required to obtain these; two simple things you must have....humility and fear of the Lord. Being humble, not boastful and being fearful. This fear is not the one that prohibits you but this is the fear that allows you to live according to God's will and command.

Are you a humble person? You can be honest because not everyone is. Perhaps you should define humility for yourself and figure out how you will from this day forward incorporate humility into your everyday living.

I Am An Overcomer

23

GROWTH

"As newborn babes, desire the sincere milk of the word, that ye may grow thereby:"
(1 Peter 2:2, KJV)

We all grow up. We get older and we are supposed to get wiser. The only way we can get wiser is by learning and learning comes from the Word of the God. Just as an infant desires its mother's milk for strength and nutrition, we as babes in Christ must desire God's Word. It provides the nourishment we need in order to grow and mature as Christian people. As with any process of development there will be growing pains to endure. However, these too are designed to increase our strength and for our betterment.

How do you desire to grow? What do you know you need to change in order to be the person you seek to be? We all have room for improvement. We are all growing.

Write about how you want to grow. As you write, think about how you desire to be better and how you think you will ultimately be able to do this. In your conclusion, include what and how you will change in order for this necessary growth to occur.

I Am An Overcomer

DAY

24

FAITH

"Now faith is the substance of things hoped for, the evidence of things not seen." (Hebrews 11:1, KJV)

Faith is something that challenges us all. It seems synonymous with trust and so many of have issues with that, right? But as we challenge ourselves to become better in dealing with every obstacle that comes our way, we must rely heavily on faith. The above scripture is one that rings familiar because we have all heard this whether we are in church every Sunday or not. But what does faith mean to you? Faith is more of an action word than it is a thing or idea. It provides for us when it appears nothing else can. What does it provide, you ask? HOPE! When you are faced with an obstacle that you have no idea how to handle, you rely on your faith.

As a Christian person, it is your desire to please God but we know we cannot do that without having faith. This faith has to be renewed and understood. You have to understand where your level of faith lies right now. How do you use your faith to not only manifest blessings in your life, but in the lives of those around you?

Write about faith. What does it mean to you? How do you want to increase your level of faith? What will this increase of faith mean for you from this day moving forward? Use these questions to guide your entry and refer back to this when that next obstacle comes.

I Am An Overcomer

25

FOCUS

"Watch ye therefore, and pray always, that ye may be accounted worthy to escape all these things that shall come to pass, and to stand before the Son of man. "
(Luke 21:36, KJV)

I tell my students to "focus" all the time. When I say it, I imagine them truly honing in on whatever the topic is and being able to think of that only. This is not an easy task because we are wired! We have accustomed ourselves to multi-tasking because there are not enough hours in the day to do it all so we do about three things at one time in order to feel accomplished. While many of us have made this work, it is not the healthiest for the mind. In order to think clearly, your mind must be free from all distraction. So talking on the phone, cooking dinner, and helping with homework may not be the best thing for your mind, even though we all do things like this. How can you focus?

Think about the obstacles you are facing and how you are attempting to handle them. You are probably trying to put out about three or four fires at once. You do not possess the "man power" necessary to do that. You need to prioritize and focus.

List these "fires" that are burning in your life (the obstacles) in order of importance and focus on how you will put them out, one at a time, so that you will not have to deal with them anymore. And even if one happens to return, you now have the blueprint for how to overcome!

I Am An Overcomer

26

SHIFT

"And I saw a new heaven and a new earth: for the first heaven and the first earth were passed away; and there was no more sea."
(Revelation 21:1, KJV)

This right here is amazing! When you reach a point in life where you believe shift is coming, you operate differently. Everything changes to go along with the shift that God has for you. You move differently, you think differently, and you definitely speak differently. The old you ceases to exist and you find an entirely new existence. This new existence becomes the foundation for how you live your life.

When faced with an obstacle, you have to believe that, not only is shift possible, but that it is coming. What shift are you waiting for in your life? How are you hoping for things to turn completely around?

Write about that shift. Start to think it, speak it, and live it. Believe that the old is passed away and that more room is being provided for the new.

I Am An Overcomer

DAY

27

PERSEVERANCE

"And let us not be weary in well doing: for in due season we shall reap, if we faint not." (Galatians 6:9, KJV)

In the midst of a storm, we oftentimes worry because we are unsure of how we will be able to handle the outcome. How will we deal with the aftermath? We have no way of knowing if our efforts will be enough. And we definitely get tired. But when we know that what we are doing is for the greater good, we are comforted by the fact that this too shall pass. The objectives we set for ourselves are based on the good that we attempt to accomplish in this life. The results of that work is great, it is often mind-boggling because they are not what we expect. We cannot accept failure as an option and still expect great things. You reap what you sow. If you sow greatness, then greatness you shall reap.

Stay the course in order to overcome the obstacle. It gets hard and sometimes unbearable. However, you are already equipped with the necessary tools to overcome, you just have to believe that you can and you will.

What does perseverance mean to you? How does it look...what does it feel like? Write about a time you persevered. Think about how it felt to come out of that situation. Figure out your formula for perseverance.

I Am An Overcomer

DAY 28

LEADERSHIP

"Where no counsel is, the people fall: but in the multitude of counselors there is safety." (Proverbs 11:14, KJV)

You may be going through a storm right now but if you can find someone to talk it out with, you may come out sooner than you think. Having someone that is a "leader" in your life makes horrible situations a bit more tolerable because you may not feel so alone. The above verse lets us know that if you do not have someone to counsel you, someone you trust, this situation could possibly get the best of you. However, if you could be in a place where the leadership and counsel is plentiful, you feel safe.

Write about someone who is a leader in your life. You look up to this person and the help or advice this person gives is extremely valuable to you. Be sure to include why this person, or talking to this person, makes you feel safe. If you have not sought this person out, please do!

I Am An Overcomer

DAY

29

ASSIGNMENT

"And he gave some, apostles; and some, prophets; and some evangelists; and some, pastors and teachers; for the perfecting of the saints, for the work of the ministry, for the edifying of the body of Christ."
(Ephesians 4:11-12, KJV)

We know that obstacles come to us to make us stronger. They also vary based on the assignment we have in this life. So when you see someone going through something that you cannot even imagine, it could be due to the fact that their assignment is different from yours. You have to believe that because your assignment has something to do with enhancing God's Kingdom, this obstacle is yours for a reason; do not ignore that!

Write down what your assignment could be. This is not easy because we can confuse what we want our assignment to be with what God has for our assignment. So you need to think about that pressing thing that has been in the back of your mind but you keep ignoring it because you feel like there is no way you can do it. That thing could be your assignment; write about that. As you conclude, be sure to include how overcoming the obstacle you are facing could be preparing you for your assignment.

I Am An Overcomer

DAY

30

REFLECTION

"To every thing there is a season, and a time to every purpose under the heaven." (Ecclesiastes 3:1, KJV)

This obstacle has not come by mistake or chance. Everything we experience has a purpose. These difficult times do not come to ruin us but to make us better and help us fulfill our purpose here on this Earth. When you take time to think about your difficult situation, it is like you are coming for it, instead of it coming for you. It has a purpose and as you take time to reflect on what that could be, you put yourself in a better mind space to handle this situation.

Write a reflection about the obstacle you had to overcome. Do you know what the purpose is? Why was this the time for you to experience it?

I Am An Overcomer

CONCLUSION

Overcoming obstacles is a part of life. We have faced them, we are facing them, and there are more to come. But now you have a formula for success. You have verses to refer to and your own thoughts to help guide you over the next hurdle.

Thank you for reading my words and allowing my thoughts to perhaps become your thoughts. Hopefully you feel as though you have been made better after going through the process of this 30 day devotional.

Made in the USA
Lexington, KY
17 November 2019